LET'S GO

2nd Edition

to the English World

4

Phonics

Double Letters

CHUNJAE EDUCATION, INC.

CONTENTS

Appendix Phonics Words
Readers
Flashcards
Stickers

Workbook

fl, pl, sl

● **Listen and repeat.** 🎧01

f l → f l a g

p l → p l a n e

s l → s l e d

A **Read step by step.**

1.
f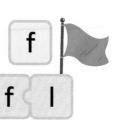
f l
f l a g

2.
p
p l
p l a n e

3.
s
s l
s l e d

B **Read and say.** (02)

fl
flag
floor
flower

pl
plane
play

sl
sled
sleep
slide

C **Point and chant.** (03)

fl   pl   sl

A **Listen and stick.** 04

1.  **fl** **ag**

2. 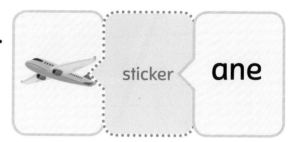 sticker **ane**

3. 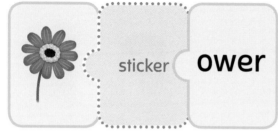 sticker **ower**

4.  sticker **ide**

5.  sticker **eep**

6.  sticker **oor**

7.  sticker **ay**

8.  sticker **ed**

 Say aloud. ❶ ❷ ❸

B Match and write.

1.

sleep

2.

ane

fl

3.

ag

pl

4.

ide

sl

5.

ay

6.

ower

A Listen, circle and check. (05)

1.
   - ✓ sled
   - ☐ sleep

2.
   - ☐ flower
   - ☐ flag

3.
   - ☐ play
   - ☐ plane

B Listen and check. (06)

1.
   - ☐ A red flower is on the slide.
   - ✓ A red flag is on the slide.

2.
   - ☐ A dog sleeps on a slide.
   - ☐ A dog sleeps on a sled.

3.
   - ☐ The cats play on the floor.
   - ☐ The cats play on the flower.

C Find and circle.

slide

flag

plane

sleep

play

flower

floor

sled

● Let's read together. 07

Ted is sleeping on the bed.

Wake up, Ted!
Let's play together!

There is a sled.
A flag is on the sled.
"Let's play!"

There is a slide.
A flag is on the slide.
"Let's play!"

Sight Words

up   let's   together   there

Writing Time

● **Write and say.**

1. fl flag

2.  fl floor

3. fl flower

4.  pl plane

5. pl play

6. sl sled

7. sl sleep

8. sl slide

➡ Go to the workbook p. 2

fr, gr, tr

● **Listen and repeat.** 08

f r → f r o g →

g r → g r a s s →

t r → t r a y →

A **Read step by step.**

1.
f
f r
f r o g

2.
g
g r
g r a s s

3.
t
t r
t r a y

B Read and say. 09

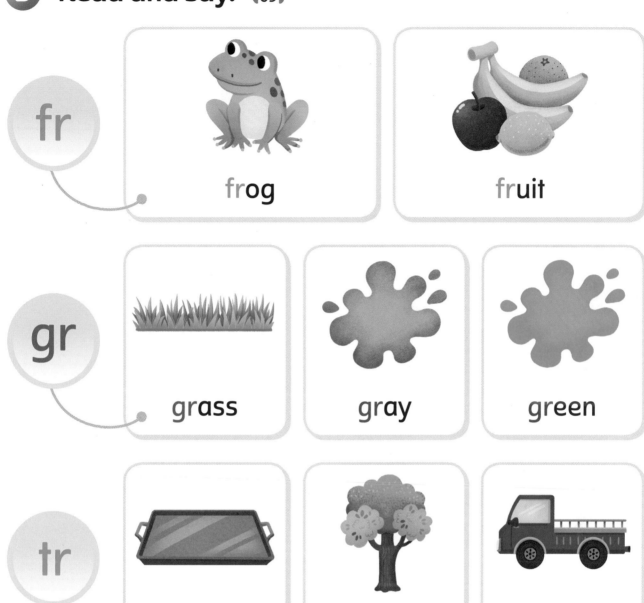

fr

frog

fruit

gr

grass

gray

green

tr

tray

tree

truck

C Point and chant. 10

fr   gr   tr

1.
fr
(gr)
ass

2.
gr
tr
ay

3.
tr
gr
uck

4.
gr
fr
og

5.
gr
fr
een

6.
tr
gr
ay

7.
gr
fr
uit

8.
fr
tr
ee

 Say aloud. ❶ ❷ ❸

B **Match and write.**

1.
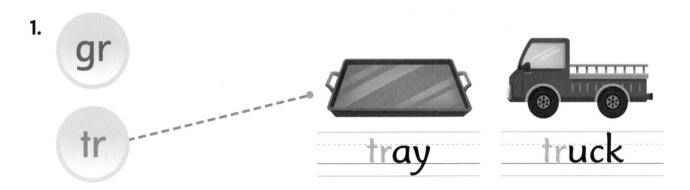

gr

tr

tray   truck

2.

fr

gr

uit   og

3.

tr

gr

ass   ay

A Listen and number. (12)

☐  truck	1  green	☐  frog
☐  grass	☐  tray	☐  fruit

B Listen and check. (13)

1.
   - ☑ A gray truck is on the grass.
   - ☐ A green truck is on the grass.

2.
   - ☐ A frog likes to eat apples.
   - ☐ A truck likes to eat apples.

3.
   - ☐ Many kinds of fruit are on the tree.
   - ☐ Many kinds of fruit are on the tray.

C **Find and circle.**

tray

frog

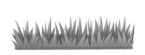
grass

truck

r	k	g	r	a	s	s	n
m	t	e	f	r	u	i	t
f	r	o	g	l	h	k	r
y	u	w	r	t	g	p	e
j	c	n	e	v	r	n	e
b	k	x	e	q	a	a	k
i	g	o	n	i	y	d	y

green

fruit

tree

gray

Let's read together. 14

I am a frog.
I can change my color.

I am on the truck.
I am red.

I am on the tray.
Oh, I am gray.

Sight Words

change   my   color   now

What color am I?
I am green now!

Writing Time

● **Write and say.**

1. ___fr___ ___frog___

2. ___fr___ ___fruit___

3.  ___gr___ ___grass___

4. ___gr___ ___gray___

5. ___gr___ ___green___

6. ___tr___ ___tray___

7.  ___tr___ ___tree___

8. ___tr___ ___truck___

➡ Go to the workbook p. 6 **19**

ch, sh

● **Listen and repeat.** (15)

ch

ch a i r

- -

sh

sh a r k

A **Read step by step.**

1.

ch

ch a i r

2.

sh

sh a r k

B Read and say.  16

ch

chair

cheese

beach

lunch

sh

shark

shell

fish

wash

C Point and chant.  17

ch   sh

A **Listen and stick.** 🎧 18

1. 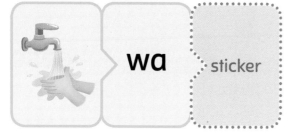 **wa** sticker

2. 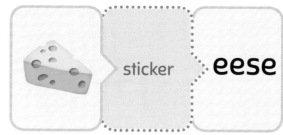 sticker **eese**

3.  **lun** sticker

4. 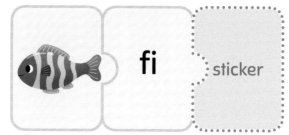 **fi** sticker

5.  sticker **ark**

6.  **bea** sticker

7.  sticker **air**

8.  sticker **ell**

 Say aloud. ❶ ❷ ❸

B Match and write.

1.

lun

2.

ark

3.

fi

ch

4.

wa

5.

air

sh

6.

bea

7.

ell

8.

eese

A Listen, circle and check. 🎧19

1.

☐ lunch
☐ beach

2.

☐ chair
☐ cheese

3.

☐ shell
☐ shark

B Listen and check. 🎧20

1.

☐ The cat eats cheese on the chair.
☐ The cat eats fish on the chair.

2.

☐ He can see a big shell under the sea.
☐ He can see a big shark under the sea.

C Look and write.

● **Let's read together.** (21)

It's time for lunch.

The shark washes his fins.

May I take your order?

Fish and chips with cheese, please.

Oh, no! It's a shell!

Sight Words

for   may   take   order   please

● Write and say.

1. _____ch_____ ➡ _____chair_____

2. _____ch_____ ➡ _____cheese_____

3.  _____ch_____ ➡ _____beach_____

4. _____ch_____ ➡ _____lunch_____

5. _____sh_____ ➡ _____shark_____

6. _____sh_____ ➡ _____shell_____

7. _____sh_____ ➡ _____fish_____

8. _____sh_____ ➡ _____wash_____

➡ Go to the workbook p. 10 **27**

ph, th, wh

● **Listen and repeat.** 22

ph   ph o n e

th   th i c k

wh   wh a l e

A   **Read step by step.**

1.

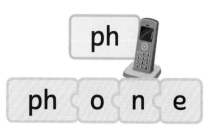

2.

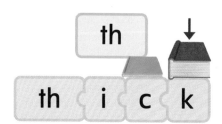

3.

B **Read and say.** (23)

ph — phone — photo

th — thick — thin — three

wh — whale — wheel — white

C **Point and chant.** (24)

ph   th   wh

A Listen and circle.

1.
wh
th
eel

2.
ph
wh
oto

3.
ph
th
ree

4.
th
wh
ite

5.
wh
ph
one

6.
wh
th
ick

7.
th
ph
in

8.
ph
wh
ale

Say aloud. ❶ ❷ ❸

B Match and write.

1.

th

ph

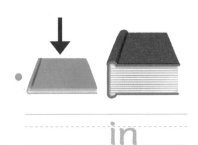

_____ in

_____ ree

2.

wh

th

_____ ite

_____ ale

3.

wh

ph

_____ one

_____ oto

A Listen and number. 🎧26

□ wheel	□ three	□ phone
□ photo	□ thick	□ whale

B Listen and check. 🎧27

1. ☐ There are three phones on the desk.
   ☐ There are three photos on the desk.

2. ☐ There is a white whale.
   ☐ There is a white wheel.

3. ☐ I like the photos in the thick book.
   ☐ I like the photos in the thin book.

C Find and circle.

white

thin

photo

thick

whale

3 three

wheel

phone

w h i t e f t h i n

s u l p h o t o v h

t h i c k w h a l e

r g t h r e e k l o

w h e e l p h o n e

● **Let's read together.** (28)

The white whale likes the moon.
She sees a photo of the moon every day.

The white whale wants to go to the moon.
She swims to the moon.

She looks up at the moon.
"Oh, no!"

"The moon is thin now!"

Sight Words
of   every   swims   looks

Writing Time

● **Write and say.**

1.   ph ➡ phone

2.   ph ➡ photo

3.   th ➡ thick

4.    th ➡ thin

5.   th ➡ three

6.   wh ➡ whale

7.   wh ➡ wheel

8.   wh ➡ white

➡ Go to the workbook p. 14 **35**

ng, nk

● **Listen and repeat.** 29

| ng | | k | i | ng |

| nk | | d | r | i | nk |

A **Read step by step.**

1.

ng

k i ng

2.

nk

d r i nk

B **Read and say.** (30)

ng

king

ring

sing

spring

nk

drink

ink

pink

wink

C **Point and chant.** (31)

ng   nk

A **Listen and stick.** 32

1. 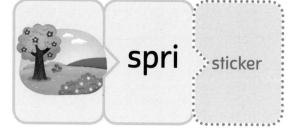 spri sticker

2.  pi sticker

3.  i sticker

4. 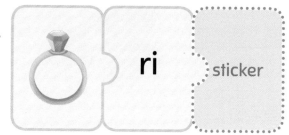 ri sticker

5.  wi sticker

6.  si sticker

7.  ki sticker

8.  dri sticker

 Say aloud. ❶ ❷ ❸

B Match and write.

1.

i

2.

wi

3.

ri

ng

4.

dri

5.

si

nk

6.

spri

7.

pi

8.

ki

A Listen, circle and check. 🎧33

1.  ☐ sing
☐ spring

2.  ☐ drink
☐ ink

3.    ☐ pink
☐ wink

B Listen and check. 🎧34

1.  ☐ The king winks at the queen.
☐ The spring winks at the queen.

2.  ☐ The boy drinks ink water.
☐ The boy drinks pink water.

C Find and circle.

ink

spring

drink

sing

a	j	s	p	r	i	n	g
d	t	i	r	p	u	w	p
r	i	n	k	h	i	i	m
i	c	g	r	e	l	n	s
n	d	u	m	i	d	k	k
k	l	t	e	l	n	o	p
g	a	j	k	i	n	g	y

king

pink

ring

wink

● **Let's read together.** 35

I drink water at the lake.
The lake sings.

I touch the flowers.
The flowers turn pink.

I call the frog.
The frog winks at me.

It is warm.
It is spring now.

Sight Words

touch   turn   call   warm

Writing Time

STEP 4

● **Write and say.**

1.  ng → king

2. ng → ring

3.  ng → sing

4.  ng → spring

5. nk → drink

6. nk → ink

7. nk → pink

8. nk → wink

A Listen and match.

1.

2.

3.

4.

pl   th   gr   ch

5.

6.

7.

8.

B Look and number.

1    2    3    4

1. ring [4]

2. sled [ ]

3. wink [ ]

4. tray [ ]

C Read and write.

floor	phone	wheel	fruit
sing	~~sleep~~	wash	drink

1.

sleep

2.

_____

3.

_____

4.

_____

5.

_____

6.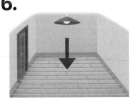

_____

7.

_____

8.

_____

D Listen and color. 37

1.

(fl) (ch) ag

2.

lun (ch) (sh)

3.

(ch) (ph) oto

4.

(pl) (tr) uck

5.

(sh) (th) ark

6.

(fr) (sl) og

7.

pi (nk) (ng)

8.

(wh) (gr) ale

E Circle and write.

1.

(nk) (ng)

 king

2.

(ch) (sh)

fi

3.

(gr) (tr)

 een

F Look and write.

flower	wheel	thin	~~ink~~
white	floor	drink	three

-nk

ink

fl-

th-

wh-

oa, ow

• **Listen and repeat.** (38)

oa   b oa t

ow   e l b ow

A **Read step by step.**

1.
oa

b oa t

2.
ow

e l b ow

B **Read and say.** 39

oa

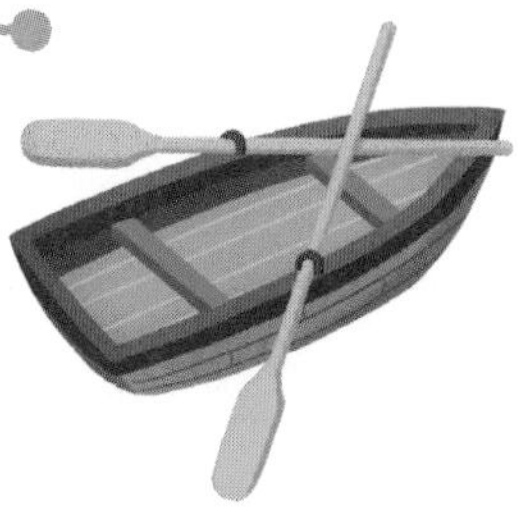

boat

coat

goat

road

ow

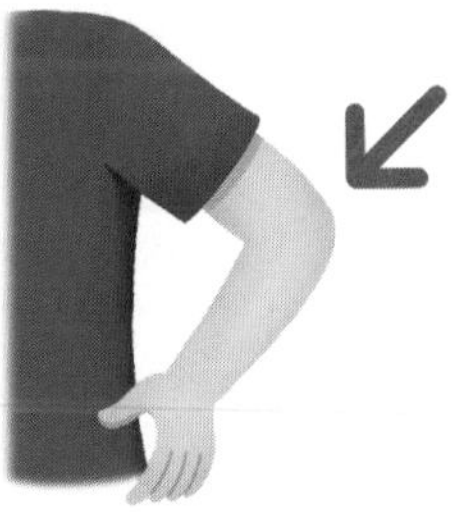

elbow

snow

window

yellow

C **Point and chant.** 40

oa   ow

1.  yell [ay / ow]

2.  c [ea / oa] t

3. sn [ow / ee]

4.  r [ai / oa] d

5. wind [ow / ea]

6.  b [oa / ea] t

7. elb [ay / ow]

8.  g [oa / ee] t

 Say aloud. ❶ ❷ ❸

B **Match and write.**

1.

oa

ow

__elb__

__sn__

2.

oa

ow

c__t

r__d

3.

ow

oa

wind__

yell__

4.

ow

oa

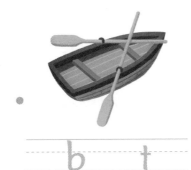

b__t

g__t

snow

window

coat

road

boat

elbow

B **Listen and check.** 43

1.

☐ The white goat is on the road.

☐ The white goat is on the boat.

2.

☐ There is a yellow coat.

☐ There is a yellow window.

C **Look and write.**

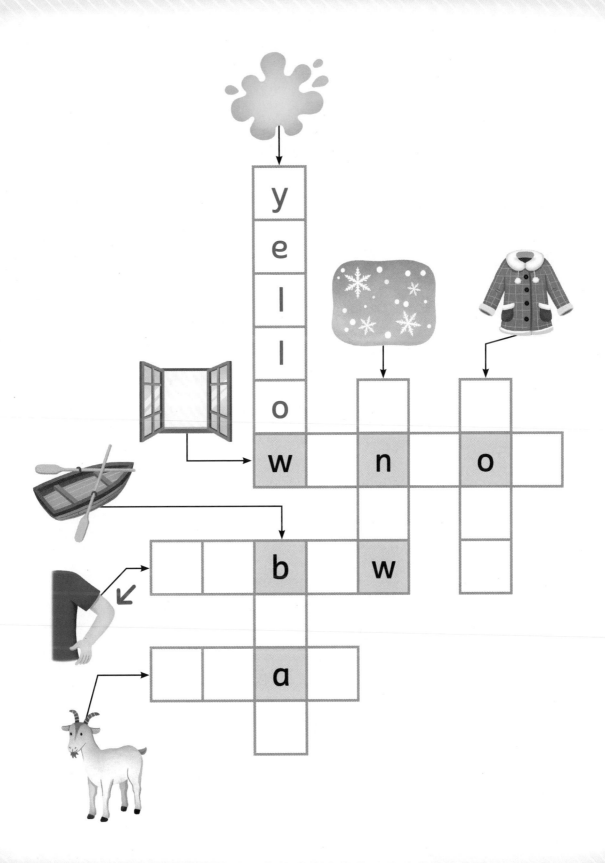

● **Let's read together.** 44

A goat and a lion are on a boat.

It is snowing.
The goat is cold.

The lion takes off a coat.
He is a goat, too!

This is for you.

He gives the yellow coat to her.

Sight Words

cold   takes   off   gives

● **Write and say.**

1. oa boat

2. oa coat

3.  oa goat

4. oa road

5. ow elbow

6. ow snow

7. ow window

8. ow yellow

ie, igh

● **Listen and repeat.** (45)

ie

d ie

---

igh

h igh

A **Read step by step.**

1.
ie

d ie

2.
igh

h igh

B Read and say. 46

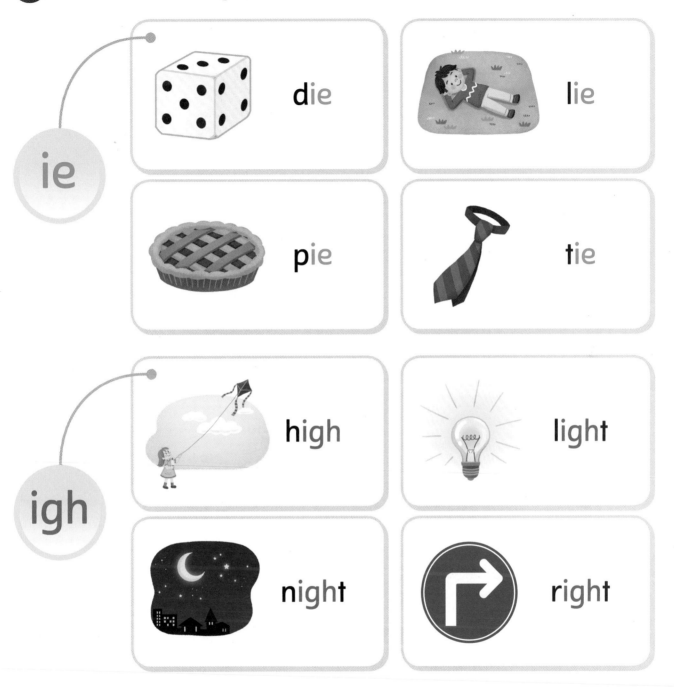

ie

d**ie**

l**ie**

p**ie**

t**ie**

igh

h**igh**

l**ight**

n**ight**

r**ight**

C Point and chant. 47

ie   igh

Listen and stick.

1.

sticker

2.

sticker

3.

sticker

4.

sticker

5.

sticker

6.

sticker

7.

sticker

8.

sticker

 Say aloud. ❶ ❷ ❸

B Match and write.

1.

l _____ t

2.

l _____

3.

t _____

ie

4.

r _____ t

5.

n _____ t

igh

6.

h _____

7.

_____ p

8.

_____ d

Listen, circle and check. 49

1.
□ light
□ right

2.
□ die
□ lie

3.
□ night
□ light

 Listen and check. 50

1.
□ The dog eats a pie on the bed.
□ The dog eats a tie on the bed.

2.
□ I turn to the right at night.
□ I turn on the light at night.

C Find and circle.

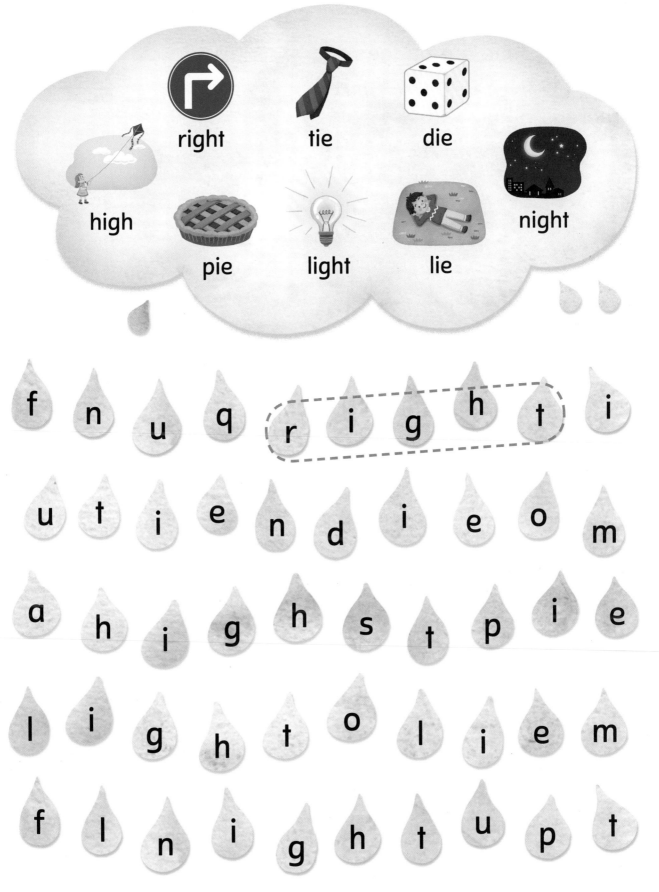

high   right   tie   die

pie   light   lie   night

f   n   u   q   r   i   g   h   t   i

u   t   i   e   n   d   i   e   o   m

a   h   i   g   h   s   t   p   i   e

l   i   g   h   t   o   l   i   e   m

f   l   n   i   g   h   t   u   p   t

● **Let's read together.** 51

Ben and Jane are on the road at night.
There is a light on the right.
There is a hut.

Let's follow the light.

I'm hungry.

They see pies on the table.

I like pies.

Sight Words

hungry follow see like

Writing Time

- **Write and say.**

1. ie ➡ die

2.  ie ➡ lie

3.  ie ➡ pie

4. ie ➡ tie

5. igh ➡ high

6. igh ➡ light

7.  igh ➡ night

8. igh ➡ right

aw, ea, oo

● **Listen and repeat.** (52)

aw	d r aw	
ea	b r ea d	
oo	f oo d	

A Read step by step.

1.
aw

d r aw

2.
ea

b r ea d

3.
oo

f oo d

B Read and say. 53

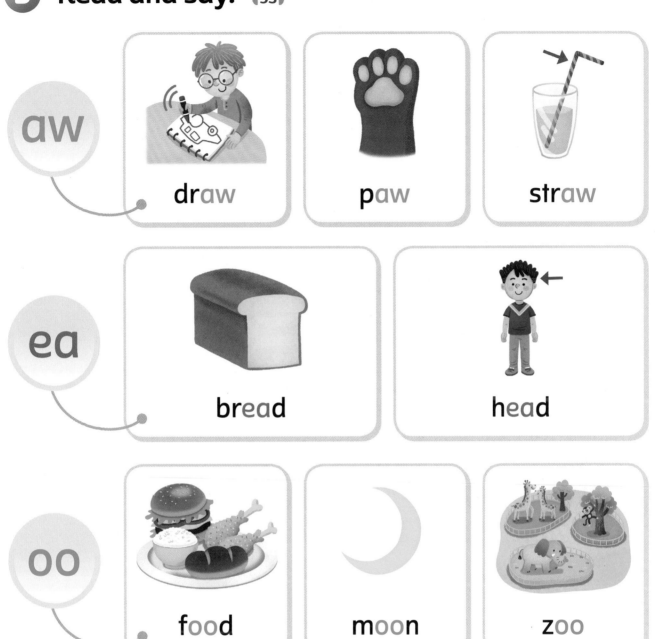

aw
draw
paw
straw

ea
bread
head

oo
food
moon
zoo

C Point and chant. 54

aw   ea   oo

1.

str — ea / aw

2.

h — ea / oo — d

3.

z — oo / aw

4.

br — aw / ea — d

5.

dr — aw / oo

6.

f — ea / oo — d

7.

p — aw / ea

8.

m — oo / aw — n

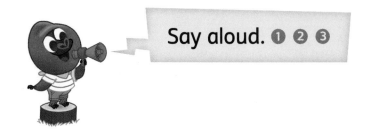

Say aloud. ❶ ❷ ❸

B **Match and write.**

1.

ea

oo

m   n   z

2.

aw

oo

dr   str

3.

aw

ea

br   d   h   d

A Listen and number. 🎧56

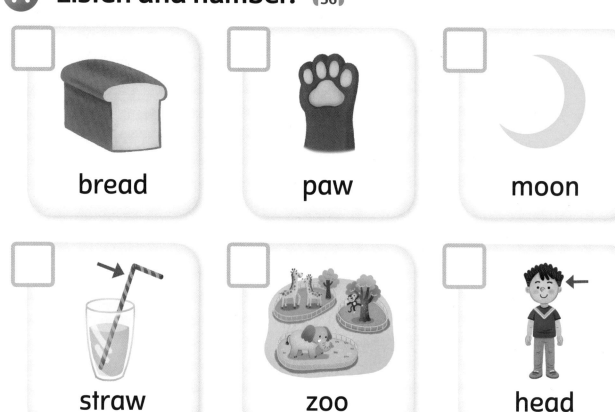

bread

paw

moon

straw

zoo

head

B Listen and check. 🎧57

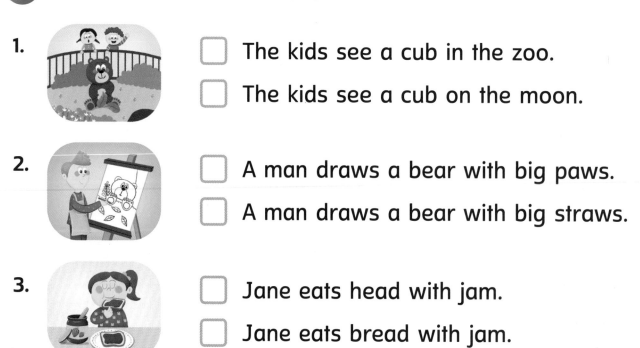

1. ☐ The kids see a cub in the zoo.
   ☐ The kids see a cub on the moon.

2. ☐ A man draws a bear with big paws.
   ☐ A man draws a bear with big straws.

3. ☐ Jane eats head with jam.
   ☐ Jane eats bread with jam.

C Find and circle.

bread

draw

zoo

moon

i	p	y	f	m	v	a	s
n	e	z	o	o	t	m	t
w	b	c	u	o	o	d	r
d	z	r	q	n	h	d	a
j	r	k	e	x	e	u	w
s	f	a	r	a	a	t	l
o	p	a	w	g	d	b	j

straw

paw

food

head

Let's read together. 58

The moon gets up at night.
She draws a rod.

She gets some food.
She gets some bread, too.

She draws a straw.
She drinks milk with it.

She is full now.

Sight Words

gets   up   some   with   full

● **Write and say.**

1. aw → draw

2. aw paw

3. aw straw

4. ea bread

5. ea head

6.  oo food

7. oo moon

8.  oo zoo

 **Unit 09**

ou, ow, oy

● **Listen and repeat.**

ou   **g** **r** **ou** **n** **d**

ow   **b** **r** **ow** **n**

oy   **b** **oy**

A **Read step by step.**

1.

ou

g **r** **ou** **n** **d**

2.

ow

b **r** **ow** **n**

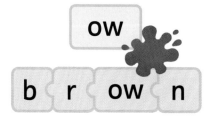

3.

oy

b **oy**

B **Read and say.** 60

ou

ground

mouse

sound

ow

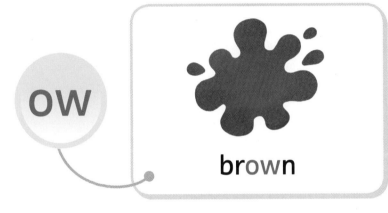

brown

cow

oy

boy

joy

toy

C **Point and chant.** 61

ou   ow   oy

A **Listen and stick.**

1.

sticker

2.

sticker

3.

sticker

4.

sticker

5.

sticker

6.

sticker

7.

sticker

8.

sticker

 Say aloud. ❶ ❷ ❸

B **Match and write.**

1.

m __ se

2.

j __

(ou)

3.

b __

(ow)

4.

br __ n

(oy)

5.

c __

6.

s __ nd

A Listen, circle and check. (63)

1.

☐ cow
☐ brown

2.

☐ toy
☐ boy

3.

☐ sound
☐ ground

B Listen and check. (64)

1.
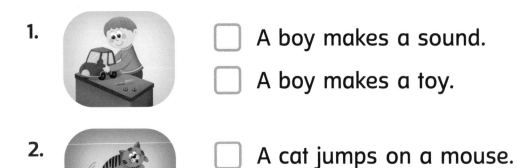

☐ A boy makes a sound.
☐ A boy makes a toy.

2.

☐ A cat jumps on a mouse.
☐ A cat jumps on a cow.

3.
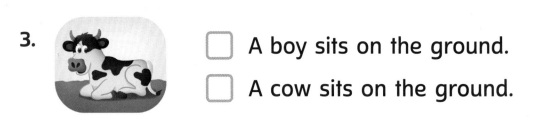

☐ A boy sits on the ground.
☐ A cow sits on the ground.

C **Look and write.**

● **Let's read together.** 🎧65

The boy lies on the ground all day.

Can you help me?

No. I want to take a nap.

Moo!

What is this sound?

I have four legs! I'm a cow!

Sight Words

all   day   help   take   four

Writing Time

● **Write and say.**

1.  ou ground

2. ou mouse

3. ou sound

4. ow brown

5. ow cow

6. oy boy

7. oy joy

8. oy toy

➡ Go to the workbook p. 36 **79**

ar, er, ir, or, ur

Listen and repeat. 66

ar		ar	m

er		s	p	i	d	er

ir		b	ir	d

or		f	or	k

ur		n	ur	s	e

A Read and say. 🎧67

ar — arm — car

er — spider — tiger

ir — bird — girl

or — fork

ur — nurse

B Point and chant. 🎧68

A Listen and circle.  69

1.

spid
er
ur

2.

b
ir
or
d

3.

c
ar
ir

4.

f
ar
or
k

5.

tig
ir
er

6.

g
ir
ar
l

7.

ar
or
m

8.

n
or
ur
se

 Say aloud. ❶ ❷ ❸

B Match and write.

1.

ur

er

spid _____   tig _____

2.

ar

ir

b _____ d   g _____ l

3.

ar

or

m _____   c _____

A Listen and number. 🎧70

girl

fork

car

bird

nurse

tiger

B Listen and check. 🎧71

1.

   ☐ The girl likes the tiger.

   ☐ The girl likes the spider.

2.

   ☐ The bird eats beans with a fork.

   ☐ The nurse eats beans with a fork.

3.

   ☐ The bird sits on my arm.

   ☐ The bird sits on my car.

C Find and circle.

tiger

bird

car

nurse

girl

arm

fork

spider

● **Let's read together.** (72)

A spider sits on the bread.
A tiger eats the bread.
The tiger feels sick.

What's wrong?

A fork is in here.

The spider comes out of the tiger.
The spider sits on the tiger's arm.

It was you!

Sight Words

sits   feels   wrong   comes   out

● **Write and say.**

1. ar ➡ arm

2. ar car

3. er spider

4. er tiger

5. ir bird

6. ir girl

7. or fork

8. ur nurse

A Listen and match. 🎧73

1.
2.
3.
4.

igh   ow   aw   oy

5.
6.
7.
8.

B Look and number.

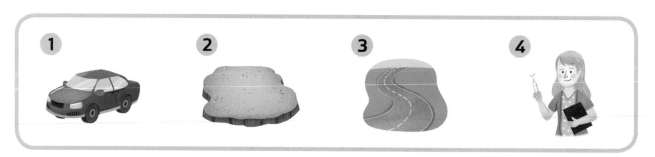

1 2 3 4

1. road ③
2. car ☐
3. ground ☐
4. nurse ☐

C Read and write.

food   fork   brown   ~~lie~~

coat   sound   yellow   arm

1.

lie

2.

3.

4.

5.
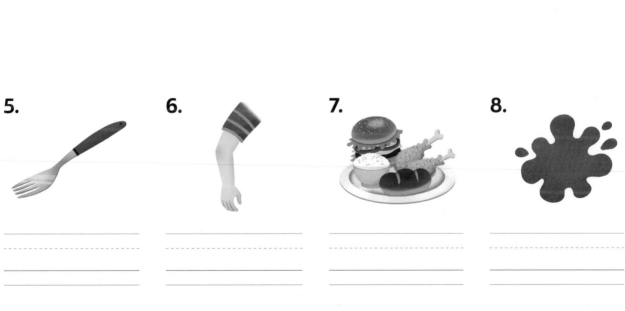

6.

7.

8.

D Listen and color.

1.

p — ie / oa

2.

str — oo / aw

3.

b — er / oy

4.

z — oo / ir

5.

c — ow / oy

6.

h — igh / aw

7.

c — ur / ar

8.

elb — er / ow

E Circle and write.

1.

oa   (ea)

<u>h ea d</u>

2.

ou   aw

m ___ se

3.

oo   ou

m ___ n

F Look and write.

boat　　bird　　tie　　tiger

die　　spider　　girl　　goat

-oa-

boat

-er

-ir-

-ie

Phonics Words

Unit 01

flag ☐	play ☐
floor ☐	sled ☐
flower ☐	sleep ☐
plane ☐	slide ☐

Unit 02

frog ☐	green ☐
fruit ☐	tray ☐
grass ☐	tree ☐
gray ☐	truck ☐

Unit 03

chair ☐	shark ☐
cheese ☐	shell ☐
beach ☐	fish ☐
lunch ☐	wash ☐

Unit 04

phone ☐	three ☐
photo ☐	whale ☐
thick ☐	wheel ☐
thin ☐	white ☐

Unit 05

- king ☐
- drink ☐
- ring ☐
- ink ☐
- sing ☐
- pink ☐
- spring ☐
- wink ☐

Unit 06

- boat ☐
- elbow ☐
- coat ☐
- snow ☐
- goat ☐
- window ☐
- road ☐
- yellow ☐

Unit 07

- die ☐
- high ☐
- lie ☐
- light ☐
- pie ☐
- night ☐
- tie ☐
- right ☐

Unit 08

- draw ☐
- head ☐
- paw ☐
- food ☐
- straw ☐
- moon ☐
- bread ☐
- zoo ☐

Unit 09

ground ☐	cow ☐
mouse ☐	boy ☐
sound ☐	joy ☐
brown ☐	toy ☐

Unit 10

arm ☐	bird ☐
car ☐	girl ☐
spider ☐	fork ☐
tiger ☐	nurse ☐

• Sight Words

Unit 01	up	let's	together	there	
Unit 02	change	my	color	now	
Unit 03	for	may	take	order	please
Unit 04	of	every	swims	looks	
Unit 05	touch	turn	call	warm	
Unit 06	cold	takes	off	gives	
Unit 07	hungry	follow	see	like	
Unit 08	gets	up	some	with	full
Unit 09	all	day	help	take	four
Unit 10	sits	feels	wrong	comes	out

Let's Go to the English World
Phonics

Readers 4

What Does Ben Want?

"Let's eat lunch."

Ben doesn't want to sit under the tree.

"Let's play."

Ben doesn't want to go down the slide.

"Let's wash."

Ben doesn't want to wash.

"Let's go to bed."

Ben doesn't want to sleep.

"Oh, you want a hug!
I love you, Ben!"

The Car Story 76

The car wants to run on the road.

But he has only three wheels.

The car meets the goat.

The goat gives a wheel to him.

But it is too thick.

The car meets the pink whale.

The whale gives a wheel to him.

But it is too thin.

The white snow falls on the road.

The car slides on the snow.

He hits a tree.

The wheel falls out of the car.

"Oh, there is my wheel!"

Night at the Zoo (77)

A girl and a boy go to the zoo.

The zoo is quiet at night.

They follow the lights.

There is a spider on the tree.

The spider is making a web.

"Look! Its legs are straws."

There is a cow.

The cow is eating hay.

"Look! It has a tiger's head."

There are birds.

The birds are running on the ground.

"Look! They run like cars."

The moon goes down and
the sun comes out.
"What a night!"

8

12

16

7

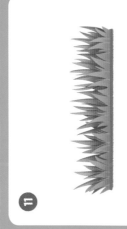

11

15

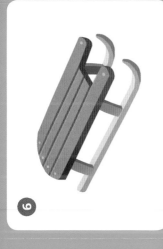

6

10

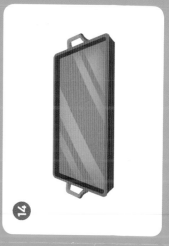

14

5

9

13

slide	gray	truck
sleep	grass	tree
sled	fruit	tray
play	frog	green

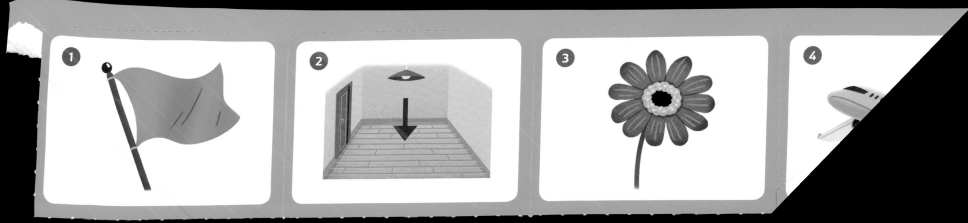

e flower floor flag

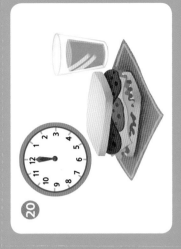

20

24

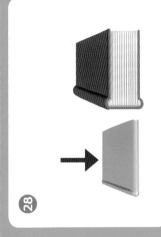

28

32

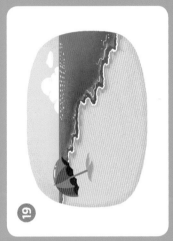

19

23

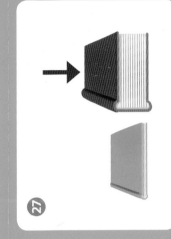

27

31

18

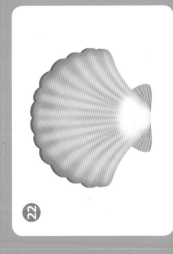

22

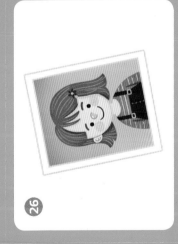

26

30

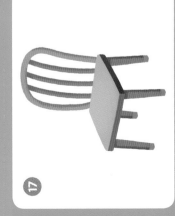

17

21

25

29

white	thin	wash	lunch
wheel	thick	fish	beach
whale	photo	shell	cheese
three	phone	shark	chair

36

40

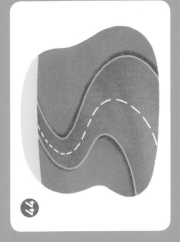

44

48

35

39

43

47

34

38

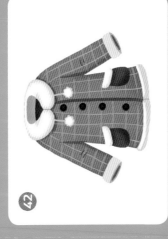

42

46

33

37

41

45

yellow	road	wink	spring
window	goat	pink	sing
snow	coat	ink	ring
elbow	boat	drink	king

52

56

60

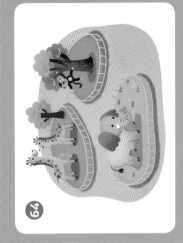

64

51

55

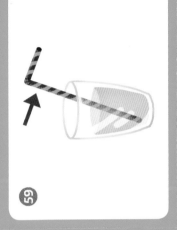

59

63

50

54

58

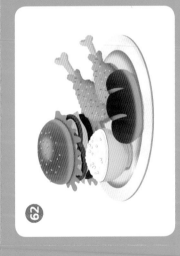

62

49

53

57

61

zoo	bread	right	tie
moon	straw	night	pie
food	paw	light	lie
head	draw	high	die

68

72

76

80

67

71

75

79

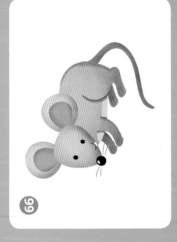

66

70

74

78

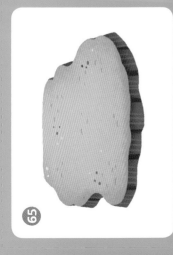

65

69

73

77

nurse	tiger	toy	brown
fork	spider	joy	sound
girl	car	boy	mouse
bird	arm	cow	ground

Congratulations!

Let's Go to the English World

Phonics 4 Double Letters

The certificate is presented to

_____ .

Signature

Date

Sticker Chart

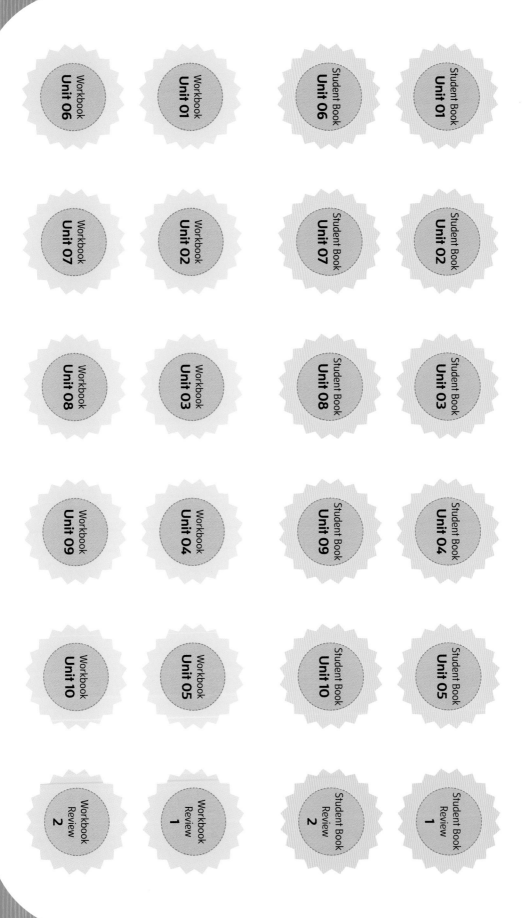

Unit 01   p. 6

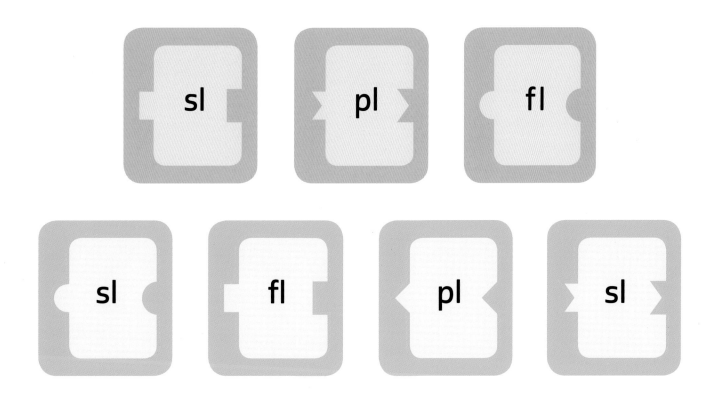

Unit 03   p. 22

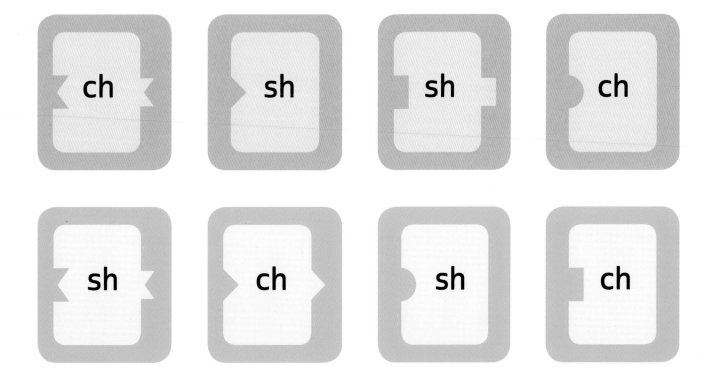

Unit 05 p. 38

nk	ng	nk	ng
ng	ng	nk	nk

Unit 07 p. 58

light	tie	lie	pie
die	night	high	right

Unit 09 p. 74

mouse	ground	joy	boy

toy	sound	brown	cow

Praise Stickers

LET'S GO

2nd Edition

to the English World

4

CHUNJAE EDUCATION, INC.

WORKBOOK

Phonics

Double Letters

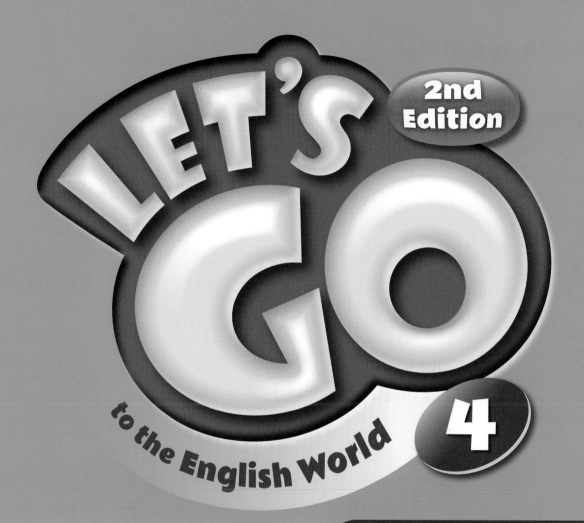

LET'S GO **2nd Edition**

to the English World **4**

WORKBOOK

Phonics

Double Letters

CHUNJAE EDUCATION, INC.

A Look and match.

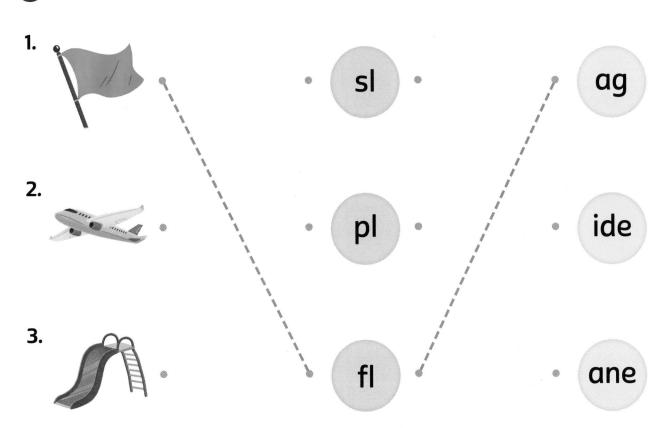

1.

2.

3.

sl

pl

fl

ag

ide

ane

B Read and circle.

1.

(floor)
ploor
sloor

2.

slay
flay
play

3.

fleep
sleep
pleep

4.

slower
flower
plower

C **Say and choose.**

1.

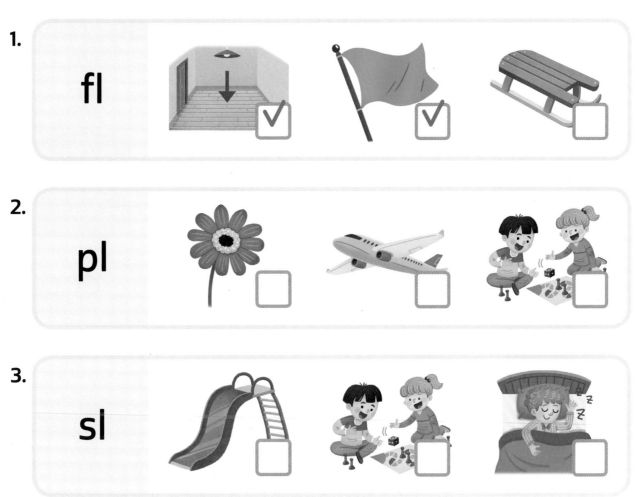

2.

3.

D **Unscramble and write.**

1.

s e l d

sled

2.

g a l f

3.

y l a p

E **Choose and write.**

fl	pl	sl

1.

p l ane

2.

_____ ag

3.

_____ eep

4.

_____ ed

5.

_____ ay

6.

_____ oor

7.

_____ ower

8.

_____ ide

F **Read and number.**

1. The cats play on the floor. `3`

2. A red flag is on the slide. ☐

3. A dog sleeps on a sled. ☐

G **Circle, read and write.**

1.  A red ___flag___ is on the ___slide___ .

   (flower / flag)

2.  A dog ___sleeps___ on a _____ .

   (slide / sled)

3.  The cats ___play___ on the _____ .

   (floor / flower)

A Look and match.

1.

 • • gr • • ay

2.

 • • tr • • uit

3.

 • • fr • • uck

B Read and circle.

1.

free
gree
tree

2.

trog
frog
grog

3.

freen
green
treen

4.

tray
fray
gray

C **Say and choose.**

1.
fr

2.
gr

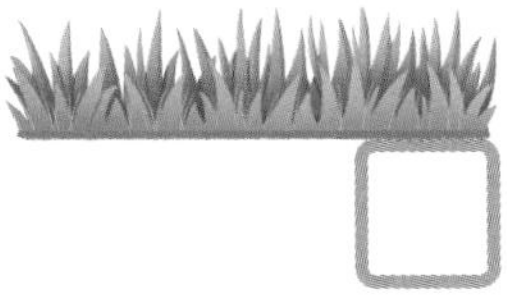

3.
tr

D **Unscramble and write.**

1.

y a t r

_____

2.

u i r f t

_____

3.

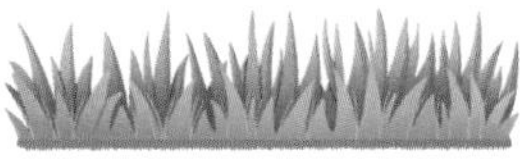

r s a s g

_____

E **Choose and write.**

fr	gr	tr

1.

_____ ay

2.

_____ ee

3.

_____ uit

4.
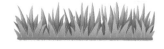
_____ ass

5.

_____ og

6.

_____ ay

7.

_____ uck

8.

_____ een

F Read and number.

1  2  3

1. A gray truck is on the grass. ☐

2. Many kinds of fruit are on the tray. ☐

3. A frog likes to eat apples. ☐

G Circle, read and write.

1.   A _____ truck is on the grass .

(gray / green)

2.  A _____ likes to eat apples.

(frog / fruit)

3. Many kinds of fruit are on the _____ .

(tree / tray)

A **Look and match.**

1.

sh   ell

2.

eese

3.

ch   ark

B **Read and circle.**

1.

chair
shair
cair

2.

pish
fish
fich

3.

sark
chark
shark

4.

deach
beach
beash

C Say and choose.

1.

ch

☐   ☐   ☐

2.

sh

☐   ☐   ☐

D Unscramble and write.

1.

h e l s l

_____

2.

a c e b h

_____

3.

c l u n h

_____

4.

s a r h k

_____

E Choose and write.

ch   sh

1.

_____air

2.

lun_____

3.

_____ark

4.

fi_____

5.

bea_____

6.

_____ell

7.

_____eese

8.

wa_____

F Read and check.

1.

1️⃣ The cat eats fish on the chair. ☑

2️⃣ The cat eats cheese on the chair. ☐

2.

1️⃣ He can see a big shell under the sea. ☐

2️⃣ He can see a big shark under the sea. ☐

G Circle, read and write.

1. The cat eats _____ on the _chair_ .

(cheese / fish)

2. He can see a big _____ under the sea.

(shell / shark)

ph, th, wh

A Look and match.

1.
 •   • ph •   • ite

2.
 •   • wh •   • in

3.
 •   • th •   • oto

B Read and circle.

1.
3

whree
three
phree

2.

whale
phale
thale

3.

theel
wheel
pheel

4.

thone
whone
phone

C Say and choose.

1. ph

2. th

3. wh

D Unscramble and write.

1. e l w e h

2. o t p o h

3. k c h i t

E Choose and write.

ph	th	wh

1.

_____ oto

2.

_____ in

3.

_____ eel

4.

_____ ree

5.

_____ ite

6.

_____ one

7.
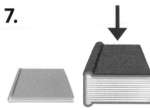

_____ ick

8.

_____ ale

F Read and number.

1  2  3

1. I like the photos in the thin book. ☐

2. There is a white whale. ☐

3. There are three phones on the desk. ☐

G Circle, read and write.

1.  There are _three_ _____ on the desk. (phones / photos)

2.  There is a _white_ _____ . (whale / wheel)

3.  I like the _photos_ in the _____ book. (three / thin)

A Look and match.

1.

ki   ng

2.

dri

3.

spri   nk

B Read and circle.

1.

ink
wink
ing

2.

sing
rink
ring

3.

ping
drink
pink

4.

sink
sing
king

C Say and choose.

1.

ng    ☐    ☐    ☐

2.

nk    ☐    ☐    ☐

D Unscramble and write.

1.

i g n r

_____

2.

k n w i

_____

3.

i r k d n

_____

4.

g i s n

_____

E **Choose and write.**

ng	nk

1.

spri _____

2.

_____ i _____

3.

ri _____

4.

wi _____

5.

si _____

6.

pi _____

7.

dri _____

8.

ki _____

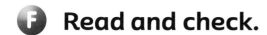 **Read and check.**

1.

① The boy drinks ink water. ☐

② The boy drinks pink water. ☐

2.

① The king winks at the queen. ☐

② The spring winks at the queen. ☐

G **Circle, read and write.**

1.  The _____ winks at the queen.

(king / spring)

2.  The boy drinks _____ water.

(ink / pink)

A Look and circle.

1. fr

2. ph

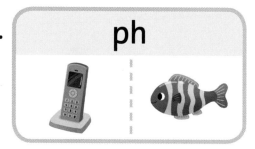

3. ng

4. sl

5. wh

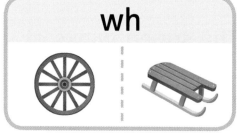

6. nk

B Write and say.

1.

__sh_ell

2.

__ea____

3.

____ale

4.

____oto

5.

pl_____

6.

sl_____

C Look and write.

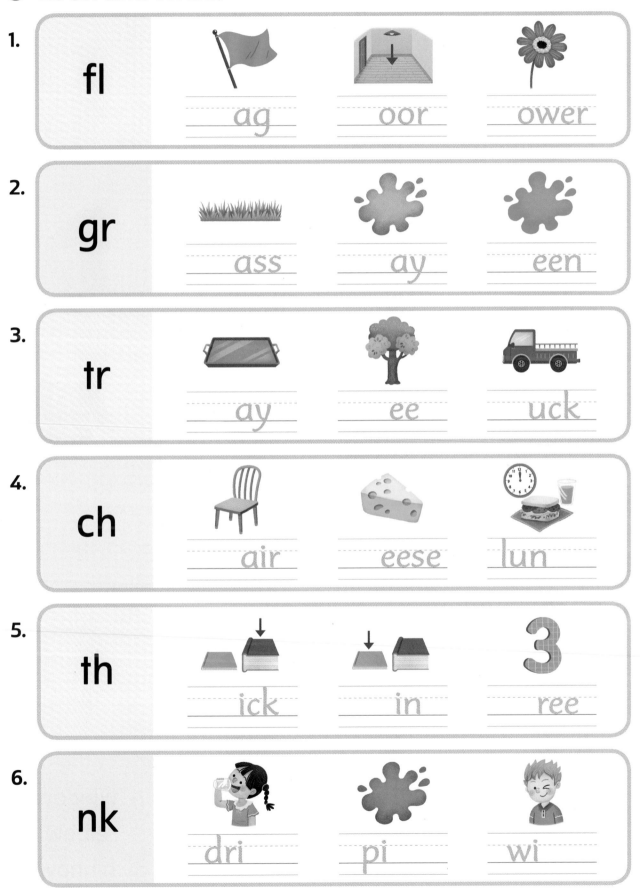

1. fl
ag   oor   ower

2. gr
ass   ay   een

3. tr
ay   ee   uck

4. ch
air   eese   lun

5. th
ick   in   ree

6. nk
dri   pi   wi

A Look and match.

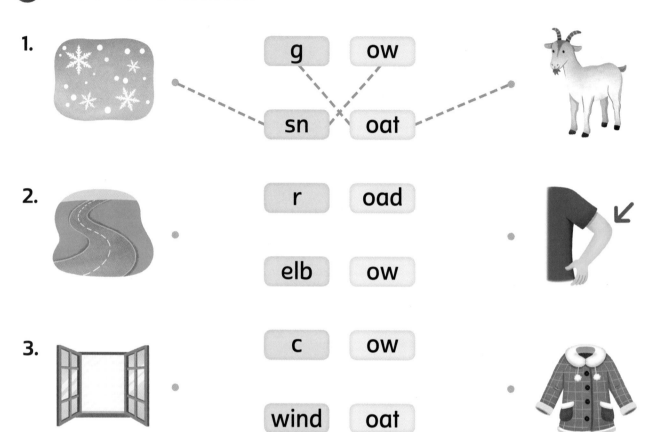

1. g | ow | sn | oat

2. r | oad | elb | ow

3. c | ow | wind | oat

B Read and circle.

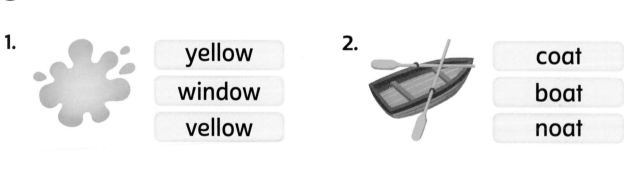

1. yellow / window / vellow

2. coat / boat / noat

3. goat / soat / coat

4. window / elbow / hindow

C **Say and choose.**

1.

oa

2.

ow

D **Unscramble and write.**

1.

o n w w d i

_____

2.

t a c o

_____

3.

b w l e o

_____

4.

a d o r

_____

Choose and write.

oa	ow

1.

c __ t

2.

sn __

3.

r __ d

4.

yell __

5.

b __ t

6.

wind __

7.

elb __

8.

g __ t

 **Read and check.**

1.

1 The white goat is on the road. ☐

2 The white goat is on the boat. ☐

2.

1 There is a yellow window. ☐

2 There is a yellow coat. ☐

 **Circle, read and write.**

1.

The white _goat_ is on the _____ .

(road / boat)

2.

There is a _yellow_ _____ .

(coat / window)

A Look and match.

1.    h   ie

   d   igh

2.    l   ight

   p   ie

3.    n   ie

   t   ight

B Read and circle.

1.    light
   pight
   right

2.    lie
   die
   rie

3.    die
   pie
   tie

4.    right
   night
   bight

C Say and choose.

1.

ie

2.

igh

D Unscramble and write.

1.

h n t g i

_____

2.

e l i

_____

3.

h g h i

_____

4.

d e i

_____

ie	igh

1.

___ l ___

2.

___ l ___ t

3.

___ p ___

4.

h ___

5.

d ___

6.

r ___ t

7.

t ___

8.

n ___ t

 **Read and check.**

1.

1 I turn on the light at night. ☐

2 I turn to the right at night. ☐

2.

1 The dog eats a tie on the bed. ☐

2 The dog eats a pie on the bed. ☐

G **Circle, read and write.**

1.  The dog eats a _____ on the bed.

(pie / tie)

2.  I turn on the _____ at night .

(right / light)

A   Look and match.

1.

str	aw
z	oo

2.

p	ead
br	aw

3.

h	oon
m	ead

B   Read and circle.

1.

sood
food
cood

2.

straw
braw
draw

3.

bread
dread
pread

4.

moo
hoo
zoo

C Say and choose.

1. **aw**

☐ ☐ ☐

2. **ea**

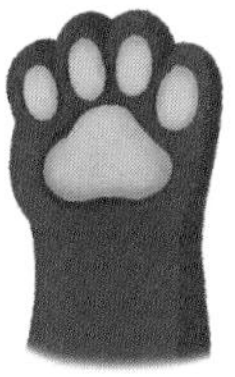

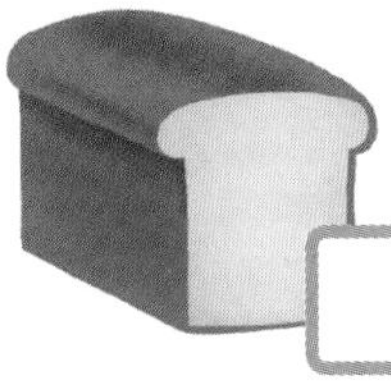

☐ ☐ ☐

3. **oo**

☐ ☐ ☐

D Unscramble and write.

1.

r a d w

_____

2.

o m o n

_____

3.

e d h a

_____

E Choose and write.

| aw | ea | oo |

1.

h ___ d

2.

str ___

3.

m ___ n

4.

f ___ d

5.

br ___ d

6.

dr ___

7.

p ___

8.

___ z ___

F **Read and number.**

1    2    3

1. Jane eats bread with jam.   ☐

2. The kids see a cub in the zoo.   ☐

3. A man draws a bear with big paws.   ☐

G **Circle, read and write.**

1.  The kids see a cub in the _____ .

(zoo / moon)

2.  A man *draws* a bear with big _____ .

(straws / paws)

3.  Jane eats _____ with jam.

(bread / head)

A Look and match.

1.

| s | oy |
| j | ound |

2.

| br | own |
| t | oy |

3.

| c | ouse |
| m | ow |

B Read and circle.

1.

koy
boy
joy

2.

toy
hoy
boy

3.

ground
bround
fround

4.

drown
brown
srown

C Say and choose.

1.

ou

2.

ow

3.

oy

D Unscramble and write.

1.

w o b r n

_____

2.

u n s o d

_____

3.

o y b

_____

E **Choose and write.**

ou	ow	oy

1.

m ___ se

2.

c ___

3.

___ t

4.

br ___ n

5.

s ___ nd

6.

b ___

7.

___ j ___

8.

gr ___ nd

F Read and number.

1. A cow sits on the ground.

2. A cat jumps on a mouse.

3. A boy makes a toy.

G Circle, read and write.

1.  A __boy__ makes a _____ .

   (toy / sound)

2. A cat jumps on a _____ .

   (mouse / cow)

3. A _____ sits on the ground .

   (cow / boy)

A Look and match.

1.

| n | ird |
| b | urse |

2.

| c | ar |
| f | ork |

3.

| g | er |
| tig | irl |

B Read and circle.

1.

arm
ark
arn

2.

sbider
stider
spider

3.

birl
girl
pirl

4.

car
jar
kar

C Say and choose.

1. **ar**

2. **er**

3. **ir**

D Unscramble and write.

1. e r u s n

2. e r t i g

3. r o k f

E Choose and write.

| ar | er | ir | or | ur |

1.

spid____

2.

g__l

3.

c__

4.

f__k

5.

tig__

6.

n__se

7.

__m

8.

b__d

F **Read and number.**

1  2  3

1. The girl likes the tiger. ☐

2. The bird sits on my arm. ☐

3. The nurse eats beans with a fork. ☐

G **Circle, read and write.**

1.  The _girl_ likes the _____ .

(spider / tiger)

2.  The _____ eats beans with a

(bird / nurse)

fork .

3.  The _bird_ sits on my _____ .

(arm / car)

A Look and circle.

1.
ea

2.
ow
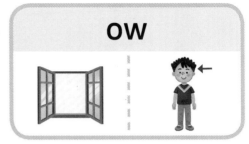

3.
or

4.
ie

5.
ou

6.
ar
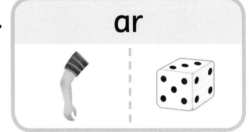

B Write and say.

1.

br _ow_ n

2.

n____se

3.

b____d

4.

__oa__

5.

r_____t

6.

____ound

C Look and write.

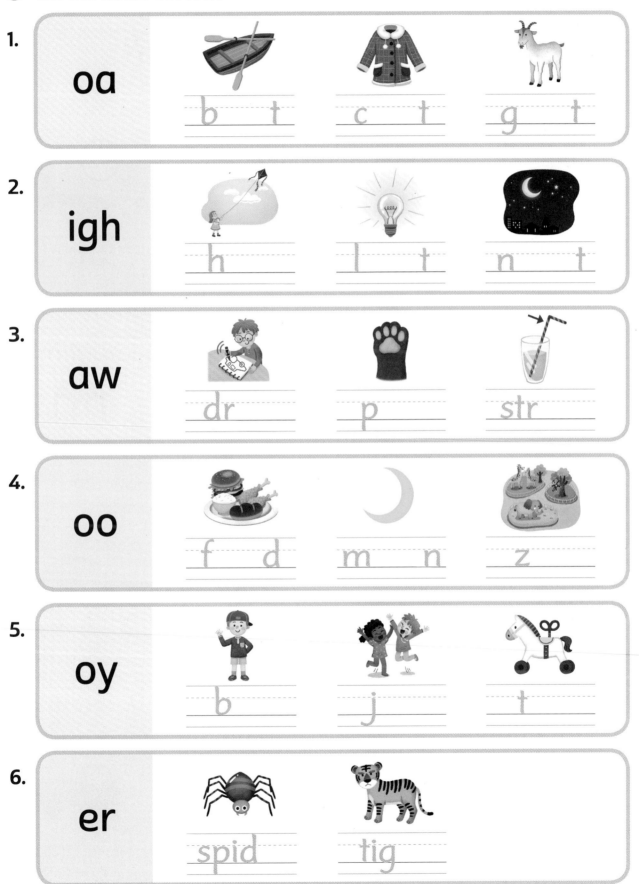

1. oa

b _ t   c _ t   g _ t

2. igh

h _ _   l _ _ t   n _ _ t

3. aw

dr _ _   p _ _   str _ _

4. oo

f _ _ d   m _ _ n   z _ _

5. oy

b _ _   j _ _   t _ _

6. er

spid _ _   tig _ _

Final Review

● **Choose and write.**

fl pl sl fr gr tr ch sh

sh**ark**

___een

___uit

___lun___

___ide

wa___

___ower

___air

___ee

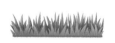
___ass

___ane

___ell

___oor

___eese

___ed

___uck

| ph | th | wh | ng | nk | oa | ow | ie | igh |

_____oto

b_____t

_____ale

h_____

si_____

_____ree

l_____t

sn_____

dri_____

spri_____

_____eel

d_____

elb_____

t_____

_____ick

_____one

aw   ea   oo   ou   ow   oy   ar   er   ir   or   ur

c___ br__d m__se br__n

z___ g__l p__ n__se

dr___ f__k gr__nd b___

f__d spid__ j___ __m